Stripping and Polishing Furniture — a practical guide

A painted door of which only the top half has been stripped and polished.

Stripping and Polishing Furniture — a practical guide

David Lawrence

Bishopsgate Press Ltd.,
37 Union Street, London, SE1 1SE

Acknowledgement

All professionally stripped items of furniture were handled by Lift Off, Wealden Forest Park, Herne Bay, Kent. We are most grateful for this work and for a great deal of advice and assistance given during the writing of this book.

©1983 Bishopsgate Press Ltd.

ISBN 0 900873 54 X (casebound)
0 900873 55 8 (limpbound)

All rights reserved. No part of this publication may be reproduced, stored in a retrieval system, or transmitted, in any form or by any means, electronic, mechanical, photocopying, recording or otherwise, without the prior permission of the copyright owner.

All enquiries and requests relevant to this title should be sent to the publisher, Bishopsgate Press Ltd., 37 Union Street, London, SE1 1SE

Printed by Whitstable Litho Ltd., Millstrood Road, Whitstable, Kent.

Contents

1	**Tools and Equipment**	**6**
2	**Choosing Furniture for Stripping**	**12**
3	**Paint Stripping by Hand**	**16**
	Childs Chair	26
	Small Pine Bookcase	28
	Bar Stool	30
	Small Cedar Box	32
4	**Tank Stripping**	**36**
	Metal Bound Box	40
	Pine Corner Cupboard	43
5	**Removing Stain and Imperfections**	**44**
6	**Minor Restoration**	**48**
	Kitchen Chair	52
	Chest of Drawers	56
	Plant Stand	60
	Dressing Table Mirror	62
7	**Sanding down, Sealing and Polishing**	**64**
	Writing Table	68
	Storage Chest	72
	Drop-leaf Table	76
	Veneered Commode	82
	Umbrella Stand	86
8	**Handles and Brasswork**	**88**
9	**Doors**	**90**
	List of Suppliers	**94**
	Index	**95**

Tools and Equipment

No very unusual tools are necessary for the basics of this work; most will already be in the average tool chest.

For stripping

Shave Hook — a wide variety of tools are available for scraping away paint. It will be necessary to have flat, pointed and rounded shapes. These will be made of steel (not plastic) and can be combined in a single implement as shown opposite.

Paint brush — for applying the jellied stripper. The brush will be ruined once used so it is best to find an old brush for this work.

Filling Trowel — for applying the paste stripper.

Scrubbing brush — for removing stubborn paint.

Coarse Wirewool — also used for removing small areas of paint which have not come away during the stripping process.

Bucket — for mixing the paste stripper and for the used stripper afterwards.

Rubber Gloves and **Newspaper** for protection.

An alternative method of stripping paint is with a **blow torch** or **hot air blower**. This is described in the chapter on stripping by hand.

1. The tools and materials needed to strip furniture by hand using the jellied or paste type of stripper.

For restoring

Woodworm Killer — there are several proprietory brands of woodworm killer such as Rentokil and Cuprinol. A supply of one of these will be essential as woods suitable for stripping are also attractive to woodworm.

Fillers — for filling woodworm holes or small gaps I use Brummer stopping which can be bought in various colours to match the wood. For rather larger gaps I use Joy Plastic Wood which will give a strong bond. But for even larger areas it will be necessary to replace wood with a new piece let in.

Glue — one of the most common faults is joints loosened either by years of use and misuse or by the process of stripping. The professional restorers prefer to use animal glues which need to be heated for use in a liquid form. An advantage of this type of glue is that it is water soluble allowing the joint to be loosened and reglued if it is not satisfactory. To-day there are several wood adhesives available which are also used with success on furniture, the best known is probably Evo-stick Resin W.

Sash Clamps and **G Clamps** — these are essential for regluing work. Glue must set under pressure to effectively bond wood together and, although expensive, sash clamps and G clamps do this job better than any other tool.

Tack Lifter to use when removing unwanted nails.

Nail Set to sink the heads of nails.

Screwdriver, Hammer, Mallet and **Chisel**.

2. Tools and equipment used most often when restoring stripped furniture.

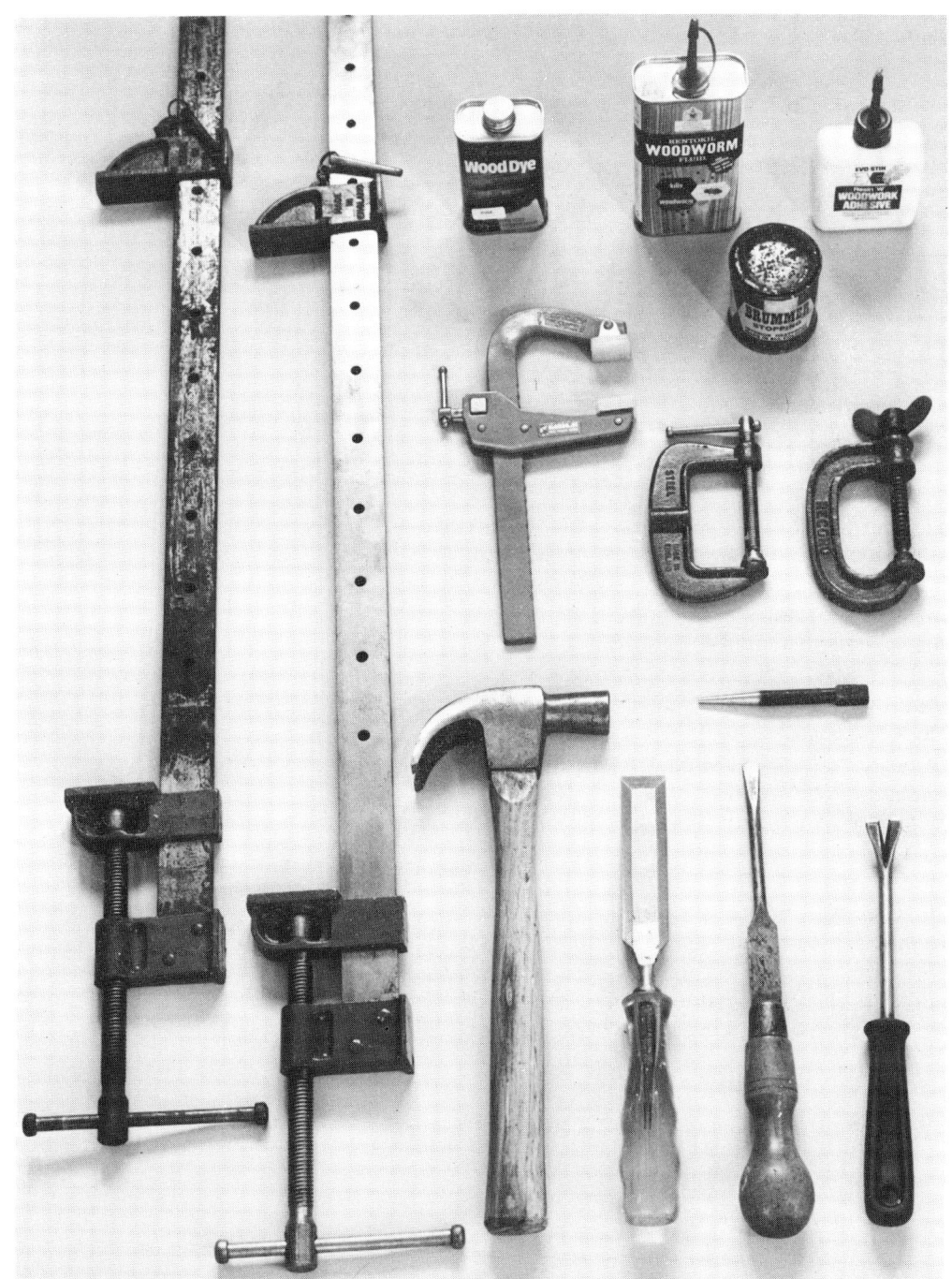

For sanding and polishing

Sandpapers — in various grades.

Wirewool — available in domestic packs and also in reels which are more economical.

Electric Orbital Sander — this is very useful if you intend to strip and polish large surfaces. The rotary sanders are not suitable but the orbital sanders are ideal for reducing the physical effort of sanding down large areas.

Electric Drum Sander — this can be used as an alternative to the orbital sander. It is available as an attachment to an electric drill. An advantage is that it can be used in confined spaces, but it does not cover the same area as an orbital sander making it less efficient for large surfaces.

Seal and **Polish** — polish can be obtained in various shades from clear to black; yellows and oranges are likely to be the most useful for pine in order to add that warm glow to the wood, and also dark brown polish for mahogany.

3. Electric orbital sander – the most useful implement for smoothing large areas.

4. Drum sander attachment for an electric drill.

3

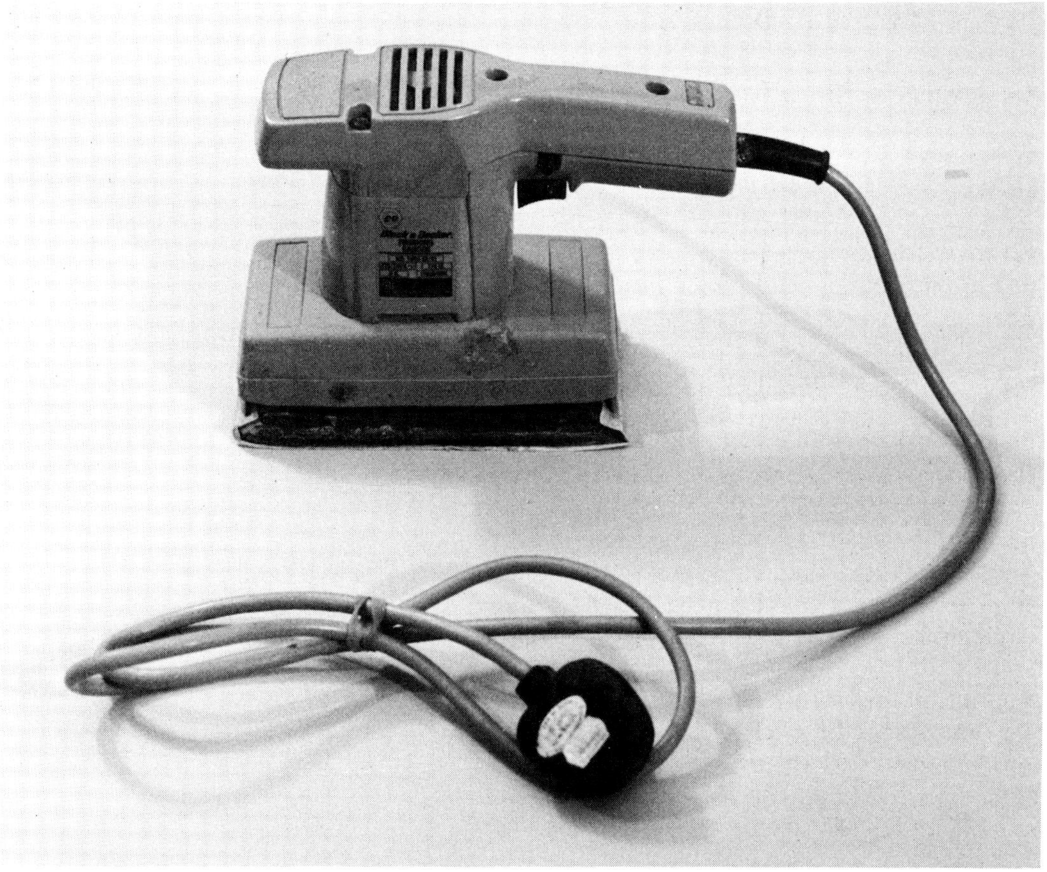

4

Choosing Furniture for Stripping

Hidden under many layers of paint is often a well made and fine piece of furniture trying desperately to get out. There are beautiful wood surfaces, which when polished, far outshine the thickly-coated gloss paint applied over the years in order to match the surroundings. Stripping furniture is sometimes looked on as 'toying with' and spoiling antique furniture. It should not be; it is as much a necessary service as that provided by the antique restorer.

Most problems encountered while stripping furniture can be overcome, but there are some pieces of furniture which are better avoided — anyway to begin with. The first is furniture made of inferior wood; these were often painted to hide the materials used which could even be rough timber driftwood or packing cases. It is important to inspect the unpainted parts such as the underneath of drawers and the inside of cupboards to determine the quality of the wood.

Secondly if you want to obtain a 'stripped' result, it is best to avoid furniture which has been stained or ebonised before painting. (Of course you may wish to end up with a stained wood when dealing with some hardwoods such as oak and mahogany). To remove stain when it is not wanted will involve work with bleach. This will add to the expense and even so probably will not be wholly successful. When choosing furniture examine those unpainted parts, or any areas where the paint has been chipped or worn away, to see if there is stain below.

Thirdly it is important to remember that several coats of paint are very useful for filling woodworm holes. The woods which are ideal

5. *Furniture in the cold stripping bath.*

for stripping are also prone to woodworm, so inspect the furniture carefully and especially those parts near to the floor — the feet of chairs and the bottoms of cupboards and desks.

You will often hear it said that you should avoid veneered furniture but this is no longer so. While it is not possible to dip this in a water based caustic solution, because the veneer will lift, it is now possible to dip veneered wood in another solvent which will not loosen the veneer. This is described in a later chapter.

Finally if you are just starting to strip furniture it is clearly advisable to start with a smallish and not too expensive piece.

6. Furniture which has been stripped and is now ready for the next stages of restoration and polishing.

Paint Stripping by Hand

At the present time there are two types of paint stripper which are commonly used on furniture. The first is the jellied type, such as Nitromors, which is freely available from hardware stores. The second type is the paste, I use Ronstrip, which is equally available and efficient. Both types are fairly expensive and the cost of stripper, even on a small item, has to be counted if you are working commercially.

These products are both powerful and messy so it is necessary to take a few precautions before and when using them:

1. Store these preparations in a dry and cool place which is out of reach of both children and animals. Reseal the containers after use.
2. Always wear rubber gloves when handling them and wash off immediately if any preparation gets on your skin.
3. In the event of any stripper getting into your eyes or mouth seek medical attention without delay.
4. Either do this work outside where it does not matter if dissolved or stripped paint gets onto the ground or protect the floor if you are working inside.
5. After use wrap the removed paint and stripper in plenty of newspaper before placing in the dustbin.

Remember that both of these strippers can affect the colour of some woods. Therefore, if you are not sure whether the particular wood which you are stripping will be affected, try a little stripper on an unimportant part to test the result.

7. Ronstrip mixed in a bucket where it has to stay for about 15 minutes before it is used.

8. Nitromors – a useful jellied type of stripper.

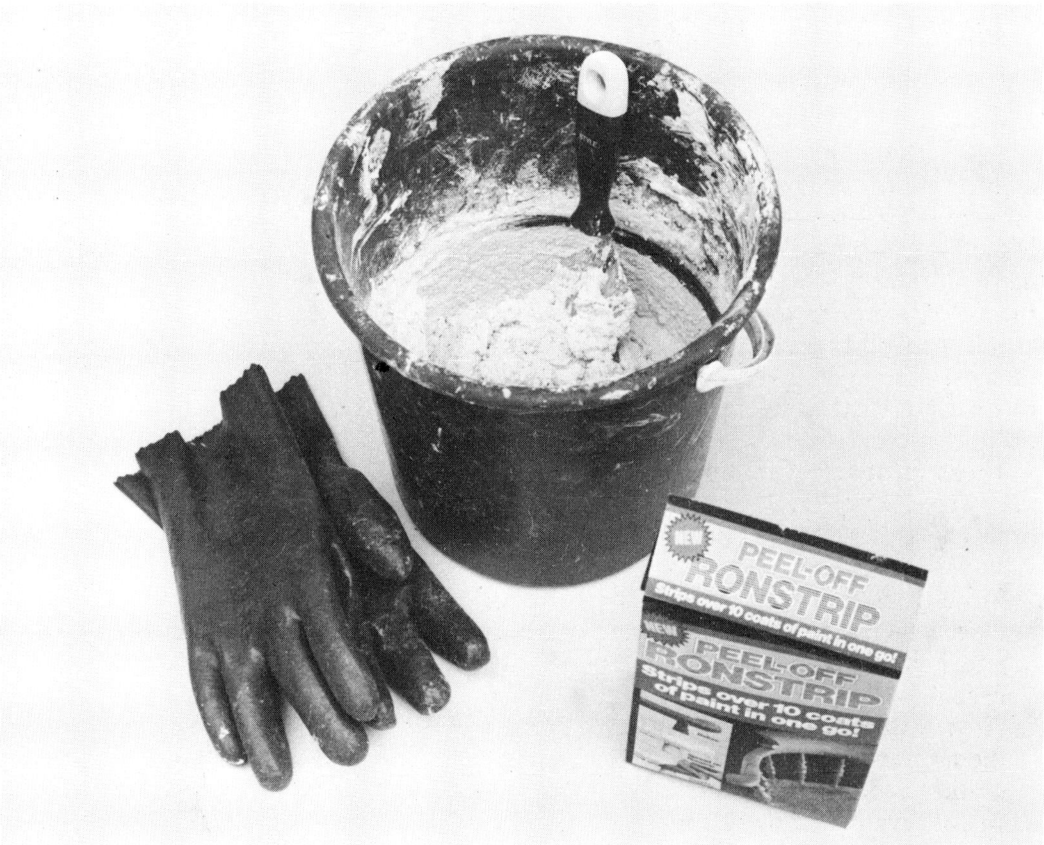
NEW
PEEL-OFF
RONSTRIP
Strips over 10 coats of paint in one go!
NEW
PEEL-OFF
RONSTRIP
Strips over 10 coats of paint in one go!

7

8

NITROMORS
WATER WASHABLE
PAINT REMOVER
FAST
SIMPLE
ECONOMICAL

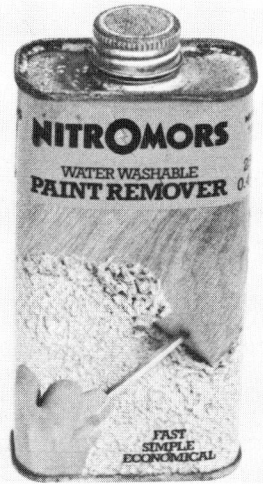

Nitromors Water Washable Paint Remover

1. Remove items of hardware such as hinges, brass handles and escutcheons wherever possible.
2. Using an old paint brush apply Nitromors thinly over the whole painted area in order to etch the old paint.
3. When the paint has wrinkled all over apply a second thicker coat of Nitromors using a dabbing action (not painting strokes).
4. After an interval of about 20 minutes scrape a small area to see if the stripper has penetrated fully. If it has not apply another coat on top of the last one and wait a further 20 minutes before checking again.
5. Scrape off the paint. For this you may require two or three implements — one for flat surfaces, one pointed and one semi-circular — depending on the piece of furniture being stripped. Some people find a scrubbing brush useful for clearing paint from crevices and coarse grained wire wool for removing firmly stuck pieces of paint.
6. Wash down the areas, where the paint has been removed, with water and detergent. The furniture is likely to take quite a long time to dry, depending on the prevailing conditions, which may even be several days. It is important not to go onto the next stage until it is perfectly dry.

N.B. When using any tools, sandpapers or wirewool it is important to follow the grain of the wood wherever possible in order to achieve the best result.

9. Nitromors being applied to a painted wood surface. Note the gloves which are essential when working with stripping chemicals.

10. Nitromors and softened paint being scraped off the wood surface using a combination shave hook.

9

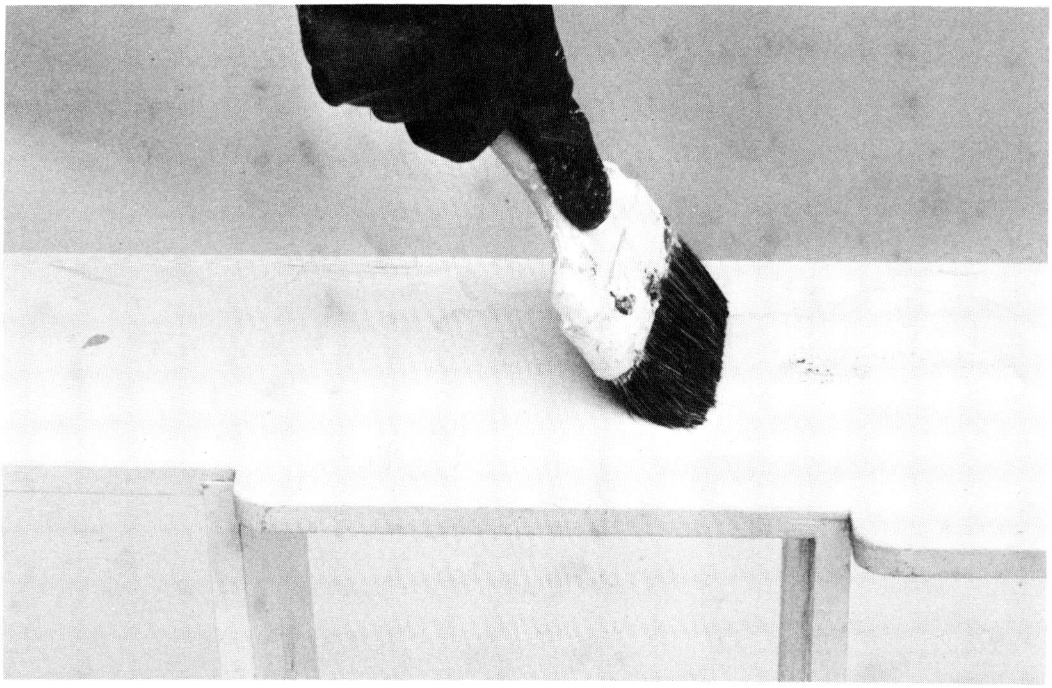

10

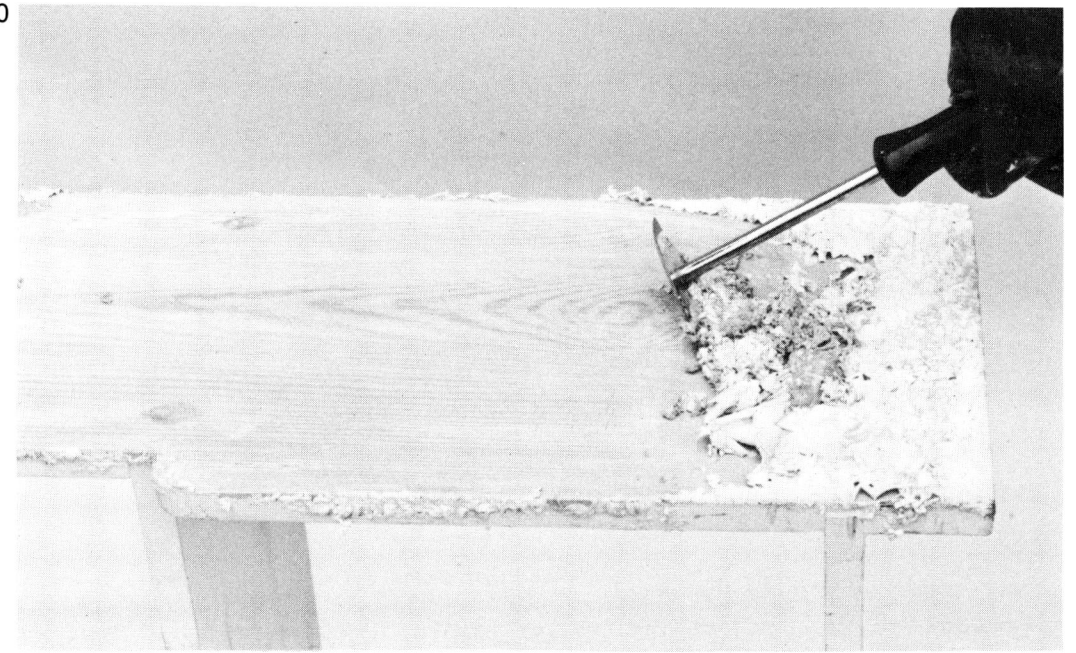

Ronstrip

1. Ronstrip is not suitable for use on all woods as it darkens some woods such as oak. If you are not sure about the wood which you are stripping the next stage is to try out the Ronstrip paste on an unimportant part of the furniture in order to make sure that it will be suitable.
2. Remove all items of hardware such as hinges and handles.
3. Mix up the right amount of Ronstrip with water (at 1 litre of water to 1 kilogram pack of Ronstrip). Pour the water into a bucket and add the Ronstrip, stiring the mixture until it becomes a paste. This paste should then be left for 15 minutes before use. Do not breath in the dust.
4. If you are satisfied with your trial apply the paste one eighth of an inch thick all over the painted areas of the furniture, making sure that it reaches down into the crevices. Do not allow any air bubbles to form. Ronstrip works while it is moist and a good tip, especially on hot days, is to cover the paste with cling film to retain the moisture longer. Be careful to apply the paste evenly all over as variations in thickness of paste will leave marks on the wood.
5. It will take two or three hours for the Ronstrip to work or even longer for very thick paintwork. It should then be possible to peel off the stripper together with the old paint in prescored areas about 1 foot square.
6. As with Nitromors remove any remaining paint in crevices with a tool or scrubbing brush and wash down the whole unit with water and detergent. It is important to remove all the stripper at one time; if small areas remain these will leave patch marks.

11. Ronstrip being applied to a painted surface using a filling trowel.

Hot Air Stripping

There is a third method of stripping by hand which is to use heat to soften the paint. In days gone by it was quite usual to use a blow lamp but today these have largely been replaced by hot air paintstrippers.

This tool can be bought at any hardware store and there are several makes from which to choose. The hot air paintstripper is excellent for removing all oil based paints or any other type of paint applied on top of an oil based paint. What it will not remove is the grain filler underneath the paint nor of course emulsion paint applied directly onto wood.

When using this method of stripping there are a few safety rules to be followed:

1 Keep the electric cable well away from the hot air.
2 The tool will become very hot so be careful where you put it down after use, and do not touch the nozzle which can give a very nasty burn.
3 Do not let paint stick to the nozzle as it may burst into flames.
4 Take care when treating wood adjacent to glass or ceramic tiles that the heat does not crack them. It is best to cover or shield these with a piece of wood.
5 Remember to turn off when not in use or unattended.

12. The hot air paintstripper. There are several makes available from which to choose.

However, used sensibly the hot air paintstripper is a useful tool and far more economical than using a chemical stripper.

When stripping paint the nozzle should be held about an inch away from the paint and moved gently from side to side over a small area. As the paint heats it will soften and blister and can be scraped away with a shave hook. This tool should be drawn firmly down

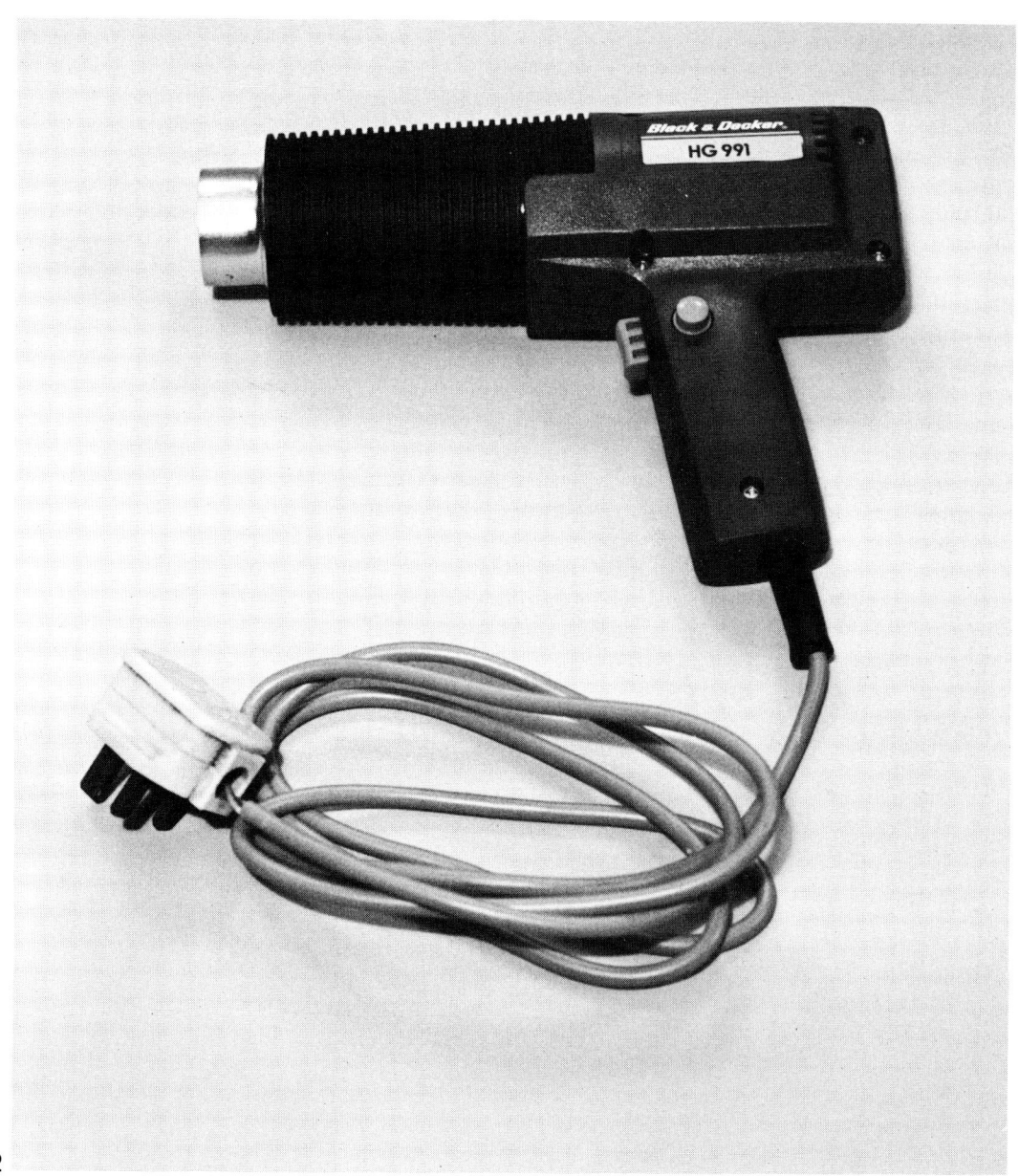
12

the area of paint removing as it goes a strip of paint as wide as the tool itself. Do not overheat the paint as this can make it more difficult to scrape off, and in fact the paint should be hot enough to scrape away just before it blisters.

To scrape away the paint use a shave hook in good condition and do not allow the paint to build up on it too much. Also the paint should be scraped away as soon as it has been heated because if it is allowed to cool it will harden again.

In all the hot paint stripper is a very useful method of paint stripping – economical, rather less messy than chemical, does not adversely affect hardwoods and provided that you have enough time it will do a good job.

13. Using the hot air paintstripper – the paint will blister quite quickly.

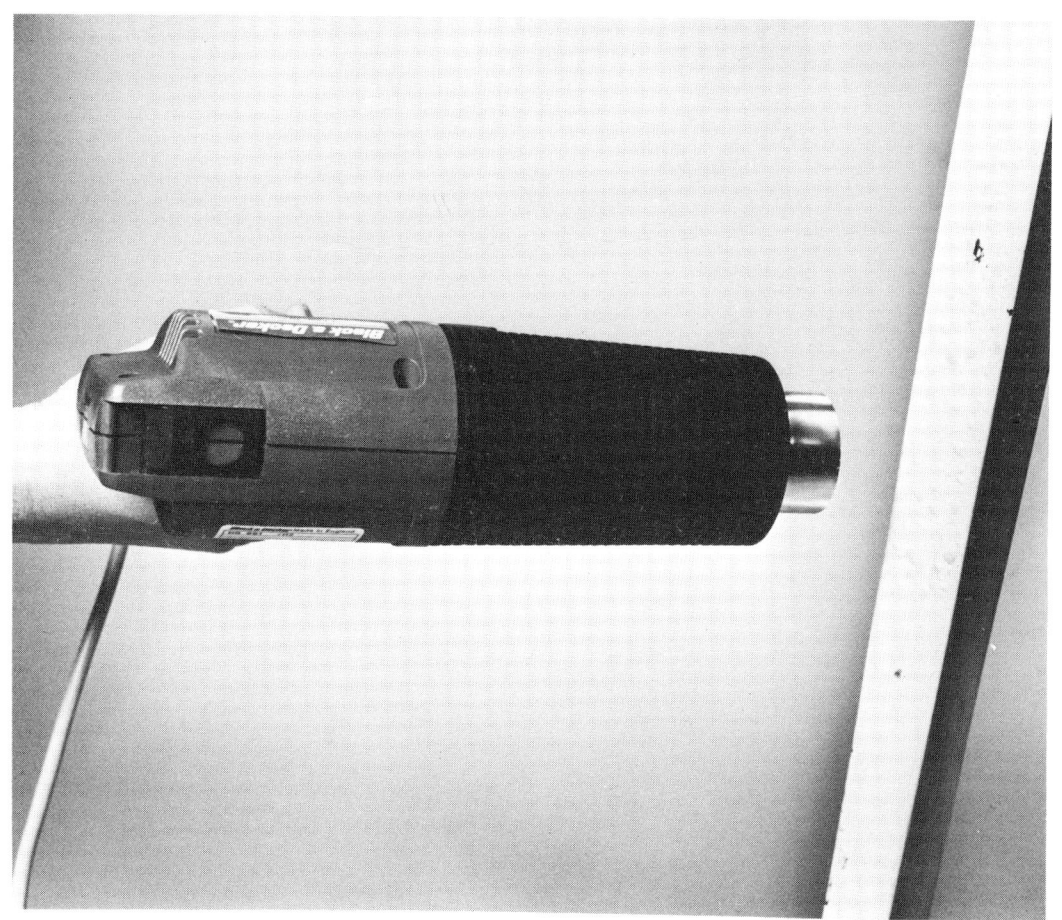

13

Childs Chair

This small chair was made of beech and was covered with green gloss paint. It was in good order and appeared to be a relatively simple job – an ideal subject for a first attempt at stripping furniture.

Stripping

For stripping this small piece of furniture we used the hot air paintstripper. There was only a single coat of paint which made the job quite easy, although it took a lot of work with the concave part of the shave hook to remove all the paint from the circular parts of the legs and back.

Sanding

The beech wood had remained fairly smooth so it was only necessary to rub down the chair with a fine wirewool in order to remove the last traces of paint and obtain a really smooth surface.

Polishing

We used a clear wax polish to produce an excellent finished result.

Because of the intricate pattern of the wood we found it better to apply and shine the wax with a brush. This way it was possible to get into all the corners and not to leave smears of wax after polishing.

This job proved to be as simple and rewarding at it at first appeared.

14. The chair as it was purchased and before any work had been done on it.

15. The chair after stripping and polishing – no hidden problems and a good result.

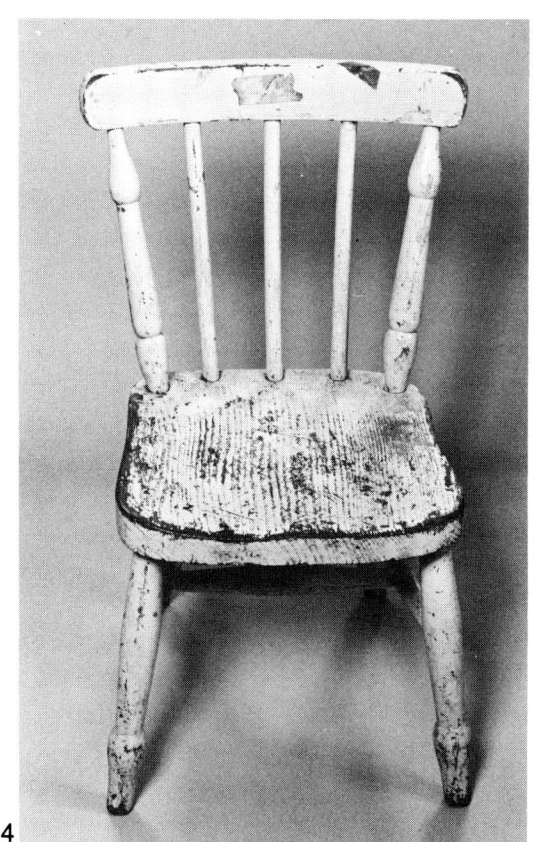

14

15

Small Pine Bookcase

This useful piece of furniture was not very old and was painted all over with two coats of paint.

Stripping

This is a straight forward stripping job with no intricate woodwork involved and of a small size. It was decided to use Nitromors. The stripper was applied with an old brush and the paint began to lift and wrinkle almost immediately. Within half an hour it was ready to be scraped off. However while the top coat of white gloss paint came away very easily the undercoat proved to be emulsion paint applied directly onto the wood. This is notoriously difficult to remove and only a part came away with the stripper leaving the residue to be removed by sander.

Sanding

We had to spend a great deal of time working on this piece with the orbital sander. Eventually all the paint was removed, but this left a slight green tint on the smooth surface although it was clear of paint.

Polishing

As a result of the green tint to the wood it was necessary to use a wax polish with added colour in order to regain the soft warm colour we wanted. The polish used was Briwax P7 which finally gave a good finish to the bookcase.

16. The pine bookcase stripped and polished shows up the grain of the wood very well.

Bar Stool

This stool was covered all over with black gloss paint and a coat of varnish but it was strong and in good order. Under the paint the wood had been stained but as we were looking for a stained result this was not a problem.

Stripping

As this piece of furniture was made of beech and oak it was best not to use a water based stripper. We decided to use the hot air paint-stripper and this removed the gloss paint without problems. As the legs of the stool were square it was relatively easy to heat the paint and immediately scrape it away with a flat shave hook while still soft.

Sanding

The wood had remained quite smooth during the stripping process so it only needed to be smoothed down with fine wirewool in order to remove some small particles of paint and to leave the wood ready to polish.

Polishing

The stool was polished with a tinted wax in order to strengthen the stained appearance of the oak and beech wood.

17. The bar stool as purchased with a thick coat of black paint and varnish.

18. The stool stripped and polished.

17

18

Small Cedar Box

This box was made of cedar and painted on the outside in brown imitation wood and on the inside with cream paint. We wanted to retain the inside paint so it was not possible to use tank stripping; however as a water based stripper can be used successfully on cedar wood it was decided to use Ronstrip.

19. The box before stripping heavily painted in brown imitation wood.

Preparation

The decorative brass handle on the top of the box was removed. The keyhole surround was made of gun metal and was left in place.

Stripping

Using the method described in an earlier chapter the whole of the box (except the bottom and keyhole surround which were not painted) was covered in a half inch layer of Ronstrip using a filling trowel. Flat surfaces, such as this box, are very suitable for stripping with a paste stripper as it makes the application easy. After two and a half hours the stripper and paint were removed together using a shave hook. The box was then scrubbed down with a brush and water to remove any remains of the paint and stripper.

Restoration

After stripping it was found that the box had a piece of wood let into the front immediately below the lock. This had been quite well done and the wood was a fair match. We therefore decided to leave it in place but to fill the slight cracks around it with Brummer stopping in order to improve the result. When this had been done and carefully coloured to match the

20. A coat of paste stripper is applied to the box using a filling trowel.

wood the restoration did not detract from the appearance of the box.

Sanding

Using an electric sander and fine sandpaper it was relatively easy to smooth the flat surfaces of the box and regain the 'silky feel' of the wood. Extra care had to be taken with the edges of the box and lid to make sure that all the paint was removed. The box was finally rubbed down with fine wirewool.

Polishing

A good finish was produced by polishing with a wax polish and giving a good 'buffing'. The handle on the lid was a new reproduction and needed to be treated in ammonia fumes in order to make it look more antique. This was carried out in exactly the way described in the chapter on 'Handles and Brasswork' — the lacquer coating was removed with paint stripper and the handle was placed in a sealed jar containing a small pot of ammonia. By the next morning the handle was ready to be polished and replaced on the lid of the box.

21. Scraping off the paste stripper together with the softened paint. The scrapings should be placed straight into the bucket.

22. Stripped and smoothed down the box is now ready to be polished.

21

22

Tank Stripping

This method of stripping is available from professionals who keep tanks filled ready to dip furniture. It does cost money but for the larger items of furniture and even some smaller items, it should not cost that much more than the price of the proprietory stripper one uses by hand. It is of course far less work for you and certainly less mess.

Do not make the mistake of thinking that one professional stripper is the same as another and that the price is the only differential. There is a good deal of know-how in stripping; the chemical baths can be speeded up or slowed down, they can be hot or cold and there is a considerable variety of chemicals which can now be used. The service offered may vary from someone who knows his business and will use the best method for the particular piece of furniture to someone else who will just drop it into a tank of caustic for a day or two and bring it out warped, loose jointed and the wood drained of natural oil.

Always ask the stripper what methods he uses and if possible visit his workshop before giving him items to strip.

Caustic Soda Solution

In the past this has been the most common method of commercial (tank) stripping but it does have some drawbacks; it tends to open grain and soften glue. It will certainly blacken some hardwoods such as oak and mahogany and lift veneers. It can however be used for pine if it is properly organised and even professionals who use cold solvents will have a caustic bath for a 'quick dip' to remove plaster.

23. *The hot caustic soda bath.*

23

Cold Solvent Systems

This is a cold chemical system based on a solvent rather than water. The items of furniture to be stripped are totally immersed in the solution to remove the paint and are brushed and scrubbed in the tank to remove the paint and polish.

Because there is no water involved this system will not open the grain or loosen the joints. Also it is safe to immerse veneered furniture as the veneer will not lift and hinges and handles may be left on the furniture as they will not be damaged. When the solvent has evaporated it should leave the wood intact with its natural oils.

In both the above methods there will be a drying period of two or three days, depending of the weather, before it is possible to continue with the next steps.

Professional companies offering a dipping service are available in all parts of the country and can easily be found through advertisements or in commercial telephone directories.

24. Furniture being scrubbed to remove paint in the cold solvent tank.

24

Metal Bound Box

This very attractive little box was well and truly smothered with brown paint which not only hid the wood but also the metal bindings at the corners.

Stripping

The box was stripped in cold solvent and then given a quick dip in the hot tank to remove the grain filler. This was entirely successful leaving the box ready for smoothing down.

Sanding and Polishing

The wood was sanded down in the usual way with the electric sander but because of the metal bindings it was found more convenient to use the drum sander. The metal bindings were also highlighted with the use of the drum sander and a fine sandpaper.

The whole box was polished with a heavy wax.

25. The box before stripping was covered in thick layers of brown paint all over the outside wood and white paint on the inside.

26. After stripping and polishing the box looked quite different and infinitely more attractive.

25

26

Pine Corner Cupboard

This small cupboard was simply but well constructed out of pine and was painted all over in light green paint.

Stripping

As the cupboard was painted both inside and out it would have been a very awkward piece to strip by hand. It was therefore decided to strip it in a caustic tank.

Sanding

The wood was rather rough when it dried so we needed to use the orbital sander with a medium sandpaper. This was used on all the flat surfaces and was followed by a fine sandpaper to give a good finish. Wirewool was used on the difficult areas to reach inside and on the crevices.

Polishing

We used a dark tinted wax polish to take back the whiteness of the wood and to give it a good shine.

This proved to be a simple and rewarding piece without any hidden problems which came up well when finished.

27. The corner cupboard as purchased and painted light green.

28. Stripped and smoothed down the cupboard is now ready for polishing with a tinted wax.

27

28

Removing Stain and Imperfections

Many pieces of furniture when they have been stripped are ready for the next stage of sanding down and polishing. But as we said in the chapter about choosing furniture for stripping there can be many a nasty shock lurking underneath the paint.

Stain

None of the standard methods of stripping which we have outlined will remove stain. In fact it is very difficult to remove it at all and dealers in this field try to avoid stained furniture.

If it is essential to remove some stain the best method to try is bleaching with an industrial bleach which is much stronger than the domestic preparation. The bleach is painted on with a large paint brush one coat after another until the colour of the wood has lightened. This method is not always successful and can produce a muddy grey tint, but it may help to lighten the colour of the wood.

It may also be possible on some items of furniture to use an electric sander to remove the top layer of wood together with the strongest stain. But stain does sink into the wood and this method is unlikely to be wholly successful.

Burns

Burns are probably the most difficult imperfection of all as they go very deep into the wood. Really the only remedy is to sand away the affected part or to replace the wood entirely if the burn is too deep.

29. Industrial bleach which can help to remove stain.

30. For a burn mark such as this the whole top of the cupboard will have to be replaced with another piece of wood.

29

30

Nails

It is quite usual to find nails in furniture for stripping. These may be there as a part of the construction of the piece or they may have been hammered in later. The second category should be removed using a tack lifter provided they are serving no useful purpose and the first category should be sunk using a nail set.

In both cases a hole will remain and this will need to be filled. There is quite a choice of fillers, most of which are suitable for this work; we use Brummer stopping. Choose the colour nearest to the wood and work in the filler with a knife or other suitable implement.

When the filler has dried smooth down the surface until it is absolutely flat and then touch in the colour with wood stain until it is a good match with the surrounding wood.

31. Using a hammer and nailset to sink nailheads.

32. Colouring the filling compound which has been used to fill the nail hole.

31

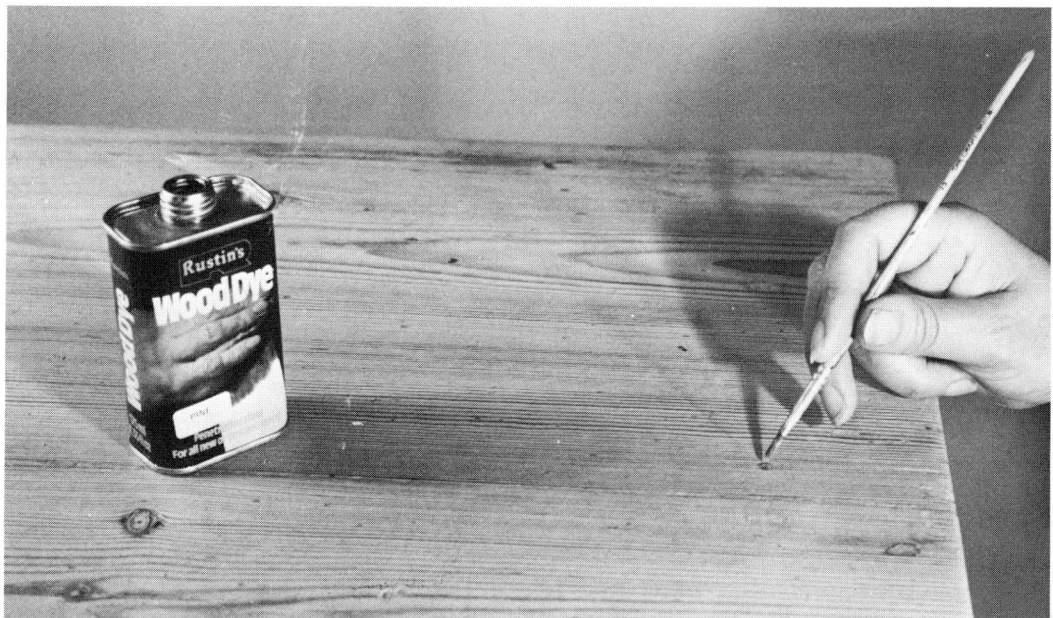

32

Minor Restoration

This chapter is headed 'minor restoration' because it has to be restricted to the most common faults which are relatively easy to correct. Restoration is a subject on which several books have been written, including 'Restoring Antique Furniture — a practical guide' by Richard Gethin — a title in the same series as this book.

Regluing

The most common fault to be found when stripping is that the joints have become loose. This may have happened while the piece has been used over the years or alternatively it may have happened while the paint was being removed. In either case it is quite easy to rectify provided you have a few essential tools with which to place the joints under pressure after applying the glue.

1. Separate the loose joints and clean out all the old glue and any dirt.
2. When the joints are clean place the pieces together to make sure that they all fit correctly.
3. Take apart, apply the glue, re-assemble and clamp the joints. If chair or table legs are involved be sure that after clamping the piece of furniture stands square on the floor as it is possible for clamps to pull the legs out of 'true'.

When fixing the clamps into position it is usual to use wood blocks so that the clamps do not mark the furniture when tightened. This may not be so necessary with a mole clamp with plastic heads. It is also usual to use some newspaper between the blocks and any glue as a releasing agent.

33. A chair which has been reglued; two sash clamps are used with two stout pieces of wood to hold the joints tight while the glue dries.

33

Woodworm

First of all it is essential to kill off any live woodworm remaining in the furniture. This is done by injecting woodworm killer into each of the holes using the can and nozzle provided. If the furniture has been stripped in a tank the solution will have already killed off any live worm.

If the amount of damage done by the worm is relatively light and does not affect the strength of the furniture these holes can then be filled in using Brummer stopping compound of the right colour. If the woodworm damage is greater but in a small area the affected wood can be removed and the gap filled with Joy Plastic Wood of a colour to match.

However if the wood is badly affected it will be necessary to remove these parts and replace them completely with new wood.

34. Injecting woodworm killer into the woodworm holes using a can and nozzle.

34

Kitchen Chair

This chair is of a variety which is made of elm and pine and quite commonly found amongst painted furniture. The back of the chair was quite badly cracked at the top and would need some simple restoration and the whole chair was painted green which needed to be stripped away.

Stripping

The stripping was done by a professional in a cold solvent bath. When the chair came out the joints were still tight.

Restoration

When the chair was completely dry the residue of paint and dirt was scraped out of the cracked area at the top of the back. This done the cracked wood was clamped together dry to ensure that it fitted together properly. The clamps were then removed again and glue was applied and worked well down the cracks. It was not easy to reclamp the back as the shape allowed the claps to slip as they were tightened. Eventually tight clamping was achieved with a mole clamp and a G clamp but without blocks. Normally one should always use blocks to stop the clamps marking the wood but in this case we had to leave them out and remove any marks when smoothing down the wood later on. However, as a matter of practice always use blocks as the marks made by clamps used without blocks can take hours to remove at a later stage.

35. The chair before any work was done on it.

36. The damaged back of the chair showing considerable splitting.

37. The damaged back clamped without glue to ensure that it will fit together correctly.

35

36

37

Sanding and Polishing

When the glue was set and the G clamps could be removed, we smoothed down the chair using wirewool until we were satisfied with the 'feel' of the wood. This was followed by polishing with a wax polish to achieve the desired finish.

39. The completed chair.

38. The back after gluing and polishing.

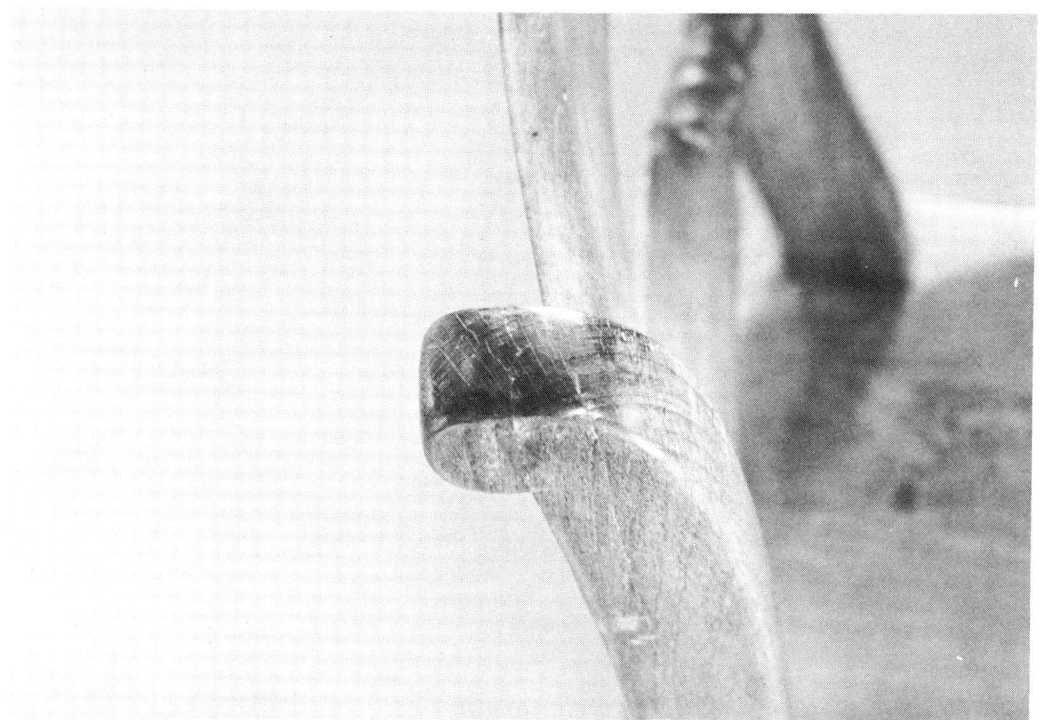

39

Chest of Drawers

This small chest of drawers was clearly used as a wash-stand as it had a towel rail on each side and splash boards on the top. It had been painted brown all over and the towel rails were loose but even in this state it was clearly an attractive piece of furniture.

Stripping

As there was quite a large area to strip it was decided to use a professional tank stripper. He stripped off the brown paint in a cold solvent tank and gave it a quick dip in a hot detergent bath to clear the filler out of the grain. This left it quite clean and ready for smoothing and polishing.

Restoration

It was relatively easy to replace the towel rails once the dirt and old glue had been cleaned out of the holes. These were glued securely back into their original positions.

One of the top drawers was found to be loose at the corner joints. The drawer was taken to pieces and all the old glue and dirt removed from the joints. When it was entirely clean and could be fitted together tightly the joints were glued and the drawer was reassembled and clamped using the sash clamps.

Sanding

There was a large area to sand down but the wood was not very rough. It was only necessary to use a fine sandpaper on the orbital sander to achieve the desired result. Areas difficult to get at, such as those around the

40. The chest of drawers as it arrived and before any work was done on it.

40

handles, were smoothed down with a fine wirewool.

Polishing

The top of the chest was sealed using a single coat of Ronseal and then the whole piece of furniture was polished.

As can be seen from the illustration the end result was very pleasing and a good example of what can be achieved when the piece of furniture you start with is attractive even though covered in ugly paint.

41. The finished chest after stripping, sanding down, sealing the top surface and polishing.

41

Plant Stand

This stand was made of stained oak and had been painted white with decoration added. We wanted to return it to its original state.

Stripping

We used a hot air paintstripper and shave hook to remove the white paint. This was relatively easy on the flat sides of the legs and top using the flat part of a shave hook. There were some areas of ingrained paint which we subsequently removed with wirewool.

Sanding

The stripped wood was fairly smooth and only required some work with 00 gauge wirewool to provide a finish suitable for polishing.

Restoration

Some of the tiles on the top surface were cracked so we decided to replace them. These were placed into position and grouted in just the same way as one would apply tiles to a wall.

Polishing

To accentuate the oak grain we used a tinted polish and this provided a pleasing result as can be seen from the photograph opposite.

42. The paint is stripped off the wood using a flat shave hook.

43. The finished plant stand with new tiles on the top surface and a good polish on the oak grain.

42

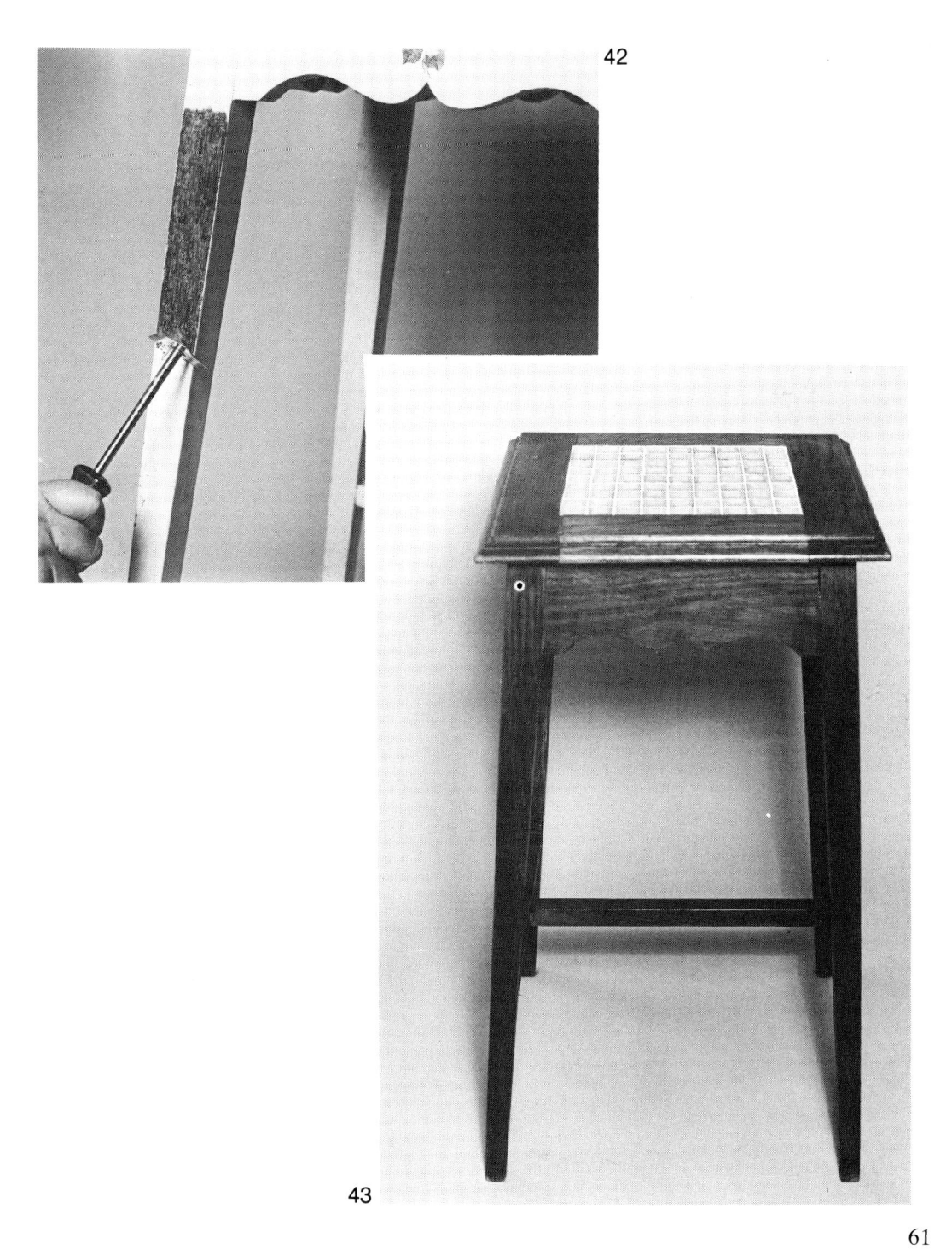

43

Dressing Table Mirror

This mahogany mirror was painted with white paint all over and was missing a foot on the front right hand side.

Stripping

First of all it was necessary to remove the mirror glass before stripping. As this piece of furniture was made of mahogany it was then stripped in a cold solvent tank. This successfully removed the paint but in so doing showed two deep burn marks in the wood.

Restoration

The burn marks were too deep to remove with the sander so we had to replace the wood entirely with a new piece. This had to be carefully planed to shape and match the other sides of the mirror and then mitre cut in the same way as a picture frame to fit correctly with the other sides. It was then glued into position and clamped. The mirror glass was replaced and the wooden back of the mirror fixed back to hold it firm.

The missing foot had to be shaped out of a small piece of wood then glued and clamped with a G clamp into position.

Smoothing and Staining

The mahogany wood was not at all rough after the stripping process so it was only necessary to rub it down with fine wire wool. We then applied stain to regain the rich mahogany colour.

Polishing

The whole piece was given a good polish with clear wax and then the two parts (mirror and base) were put back together to make an attractive dressing table mirror.

44. The mirror as it arrived – painted white and missing a foot.

45. After stripping the burn marks became obvious.

46. The wood with the marks and the foot have been replaced and the mirror is now ready to be stained and polished.

44

45

46

63

Sanding Down, Sealing and Polishing

The stripping process is bound to roughen the surface of the wood to some degree. When pine is being stripped in a caustic bath the resulting surface will be very rough but where a harder wood such as beech is stripped in a cold solvent bath the surface will need only a fine rub down.

For the rougher surfaces use a medium grade sandpaper by hand or on an orbital sander in order to remove the worst of the roughness. Then follow this with a fine sandpaper. For shaped surfaces such as the turned legs of a chair it will probably by more convenient to use wirewool (0 or 00 guage).

Where items of furniture have remained fairly smooth while being stripped it may be possible to use only a fine wirewool to regain the original 'silky' feeling of the surface.

Sealing

Where a working surface such as a table top or the top of a dresser base, has been stripped it is necessary to seal the surface so that it will not mark when spilled food or hot dishes are placed on it.

To provide an effective seal a mixture of 50% Ronseal and 50% white spirit is painted liberally over the surface. This will sink into the bare wood and should be left for 24 hours to dry. The wood is then sanded down with a fine sandpaper and a further coat of 100% Ronseal applied.

This should be adequate for an ordinary table but, if hot dishes are likely to be placed

47. The orbital sander being used on a table top.

48. The drum sander here is smoothing the surface of a large box.

47

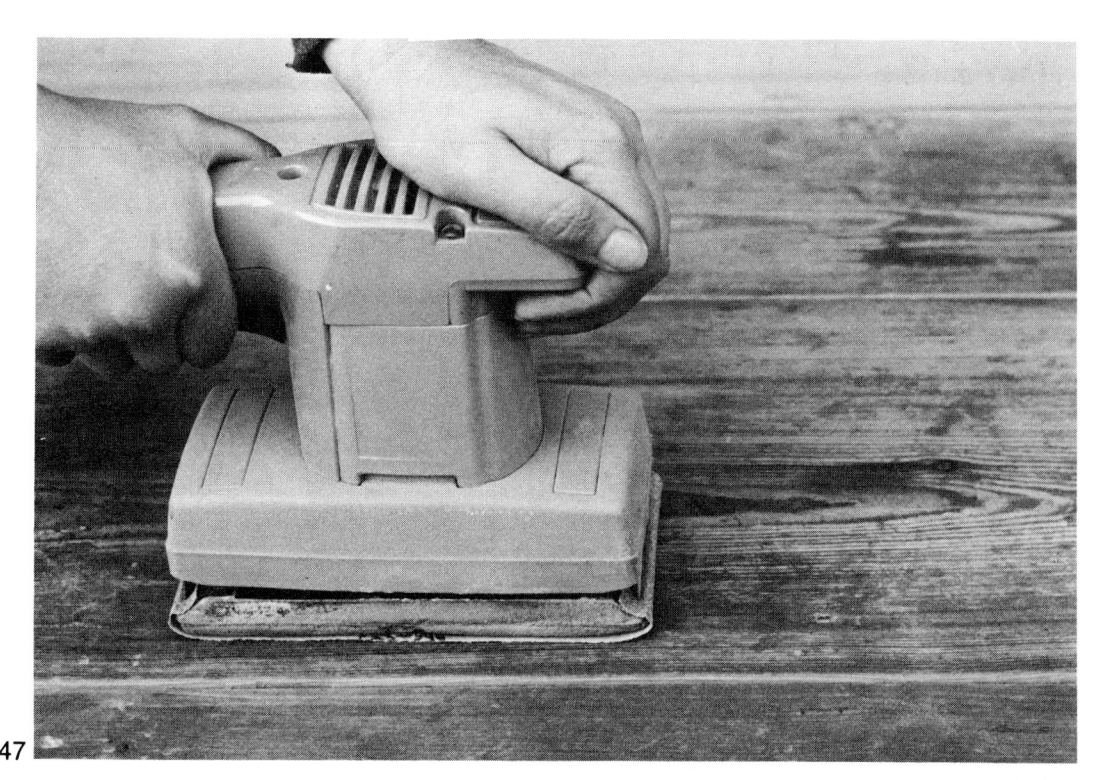

48

on it, the surface should receive a third layer of the Ronseal.

Some people then like to add a wax polish and there is no harm in doing this if you think that it helps.

Polishing

Whether or not the wood has been sealed it will all need to be polished.

There is no great secret in polishing; it is just straight forward hard work which provides the warm and glowing result which is so attractive and popular. A heavy wax will be best for the job which will use up a surprisingly large quantity. For this reason it can be useful and a saving to buy polish in the big three or four litre cans rather than use several small domestic tins of polish.

It is also possible to obtain polish in various shades and colours. If you intend to strip and polish a lot of furniture it is worthwhile to experiment with these and keep some tins of the ones which you like best at hand

When applying polish remember that you can use not only a cloth but also a brush. This may sound rather obvious but many people seem to forget that a brush will be able to get into all the crevices where smears of polish are likely to be left by a cloth.

49. Using wirewool to smooth down the leg of a chair.

50. Wirewool being used on a flat surface.

51. Some seal and wax polish which we use.

49

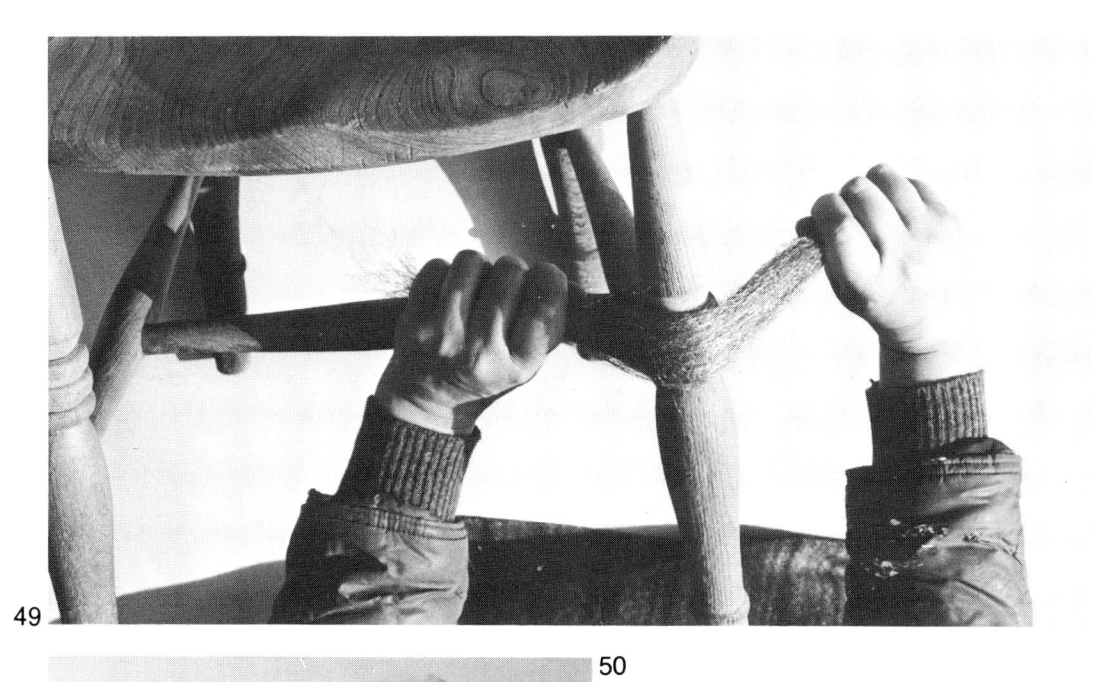

50

51

Writing Table

This pine writing table had been used as a work bench and there was a piece of hardboard nailed to the top surface. Three of the four handles were missing.

It was necessary first of all to remove the hardboard from the top. This revealed some badly damaged mahogany veneer around the outside of the top surface. We decided to remove this and to restore the pine surface.

Stripping

First of all the table was dipped in a cold solvent tank in order to remove the paint and this was followed by a quick dip in the caustic tank to remove the grain filler. The veneer also came away easily in the caustic tank.

52. The writing table before any work was done on it.

53. A loose joint to one of the table legs causing a gap on the top surface.

54. The loose joint glued and clamped.

52

53

54

Restoration

One leg joint was loose and this was glued and clamped back into position with a sash clamp and wood blocks. There were also several nail holes in the top surface which were filled with Brummer stopping and coloured after sanding to match the wood. The handles were replaced with china knobs which suited this fairly delicate piece of furniture rather well.

The drawers were too tight and were sanded down with the drum sander in order to make them run smoothly and we had to replace two of the drawer stops which were missing.

Sanding

A great deal of sanding was necessary on the top surface as it was in bad condition, starting with a coarse grade sandpaper and following with a medium grade on the orbital sander. The legs were also rough and these were treated on the flat surfaces with the sander and on the shaped areas with wirewool.

Polishing

The wood had become rather white as a result of so much sanding down so a wax polish with some added colour (Briwax P7) was used. This gave a very pleasing final result.

55. The finished table sealed on the top surface, polished all over and with new ceramic drawer knobs.

55

Storage Chest

This chest when new was probably used to store silver and valuable items which needed to be locked away. The inside was elaborately made of mahogany with inlay and divided into separate boxes. A small amount of restoration was necessary on the inlay as some of it had lifted but in general the chest was in good condition.

Stripping

As the inside of the chest was lined with a mahogany veneer this piece of furniture had to be stripped in a solution which did not contain water. It was therefore given to a professional stripper to put in a cold solvent tank.

56. The box before stripping.

The outside of the chest was painted with a grey gloss paint which came away quite easily. But underneath this was a coat of black paint from which a black stain had penetrated the wood; this was difficult to remove and required further time in the tank.

Restoration

When dry the chest was in fact well stripped with no trace of the black stain left. However the stripping time had weakened the glued joints between the planks of wood which made up the sides. It was necessary therefore to reglue and sash clamp these before proceeding with the sanding down.

Some restoration was also needed to the inlay on the boxes. This was not connected with stripping process as the boxes were not stripped. It was not in fact a difficult job; we cleaned the dirt and old glue away from underneath the veneer which had lifted, carefully squeezed in new glue and clamped the piece for the glue to set. Please note in the illustration that it is essential to use wood

57. Veneer being reglued and clamped on one of the internal boxes.

56

57

blocks and paper to prevent the clamps marking the veneer and to stop the glue, seeping out under pressure, from glueing up the blocks.

Sanding

This chest was a large area and took a long time to smooth down properly but the method was much the same; the orbital sander was used on the open areas, the drum sander saved a great deal of time in the corners and wirewool was used in areas which the sanders could not reach.

Polishing

The wood had become lightened by the time it spent in the stripping solution and as this was an old piece of furniture we wanted to darken it again. We therefore used a dark tinted wax which gave the wood a more natural look and did not make it contrast too much with the mahogany parts of the chest.

58. The completed job.

58

Drop-leaf Table

The top and leaves of this kitchen table had not been painted although the frame and legs were covered with a single coat of brown paint. There was a gap between the two planks making up the table top which required closing.

Restoration

The top was taken off the frame quite simply by tapping it on the underside with a mallet and wood block until the nails securing it pulled out of the frame. This came away easily.

It was then necessary to remove the small supporting pieces at each end of the top in order to free the two boards. This done, the edges of the boards were scraped to remove all the dirt and old glue which had accumulated over the years.

Glue was then applied to the board edges and the sash clamps were used to apply light pressure to hold the boards together. The end supporting pieces were replaced (glued and nailed as before) and held by G clamps to stop the top bowing. The sash clamps were then fully tightened.

The glue was allowed to harden overnight and the next day the top was ready to be replaced onto the frame.

Stripping

Before replacing the table top it was clearly convenient to strip the paint off the legs and frame. This was done by using Nitromors as described in an earlier chapter.

The jelly was applied using an old paint brush and making sure that it was worked well into the crevices. After 20 minutes it was possible to scrape off the paint using a combina-

59. The table before any work was done on it. The legs are painted dark brown.

60. It is quite usual to find a split between the planks making up the top of a table.

59

60

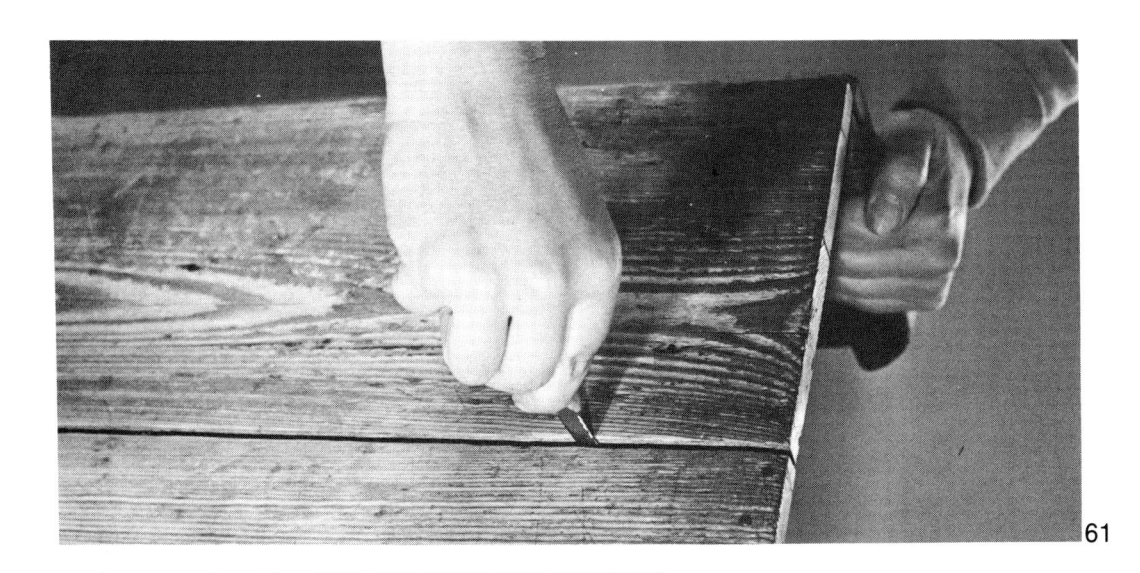

61. Cleaning dry glue and dirt out of the gap in the top surface.

62. Sash clamps and G clamps are used to hold the table top firmly while the glue is drying.

63. Applying Nitromors to the painted area of the table.

64. Scraping off the stripper and paint with a shave hook.

79

tion shave hook. The frame and legs were then scrubbed with a scrubbing brush and water to remove any deep-seated paint and to neutralise the stripping agent. Finally any spots of remaining paint were removed by rubbing with a piece of coarse wirewool.

The table was left for several days so that the wood dried out completely.

Sanding

On a large area such as this table it is essential to use an electric sander.

First of all the legs were sanded down using the sander on the flat areas and wirewool in the crevices. The top was then replaced and all the nail heads sunk below the surface of the wood using a hammer and nail set. The electric sander was then used to treat the whole top surface of the table and the edges.

When the surface was absolutely flat and smooth, the filler in the nail holes was then coloured with wood stain so that it exactly matched the wood of the table top.

Polishing and Sealing

To seal the top working surface of the table a mixture of half white spirit and half Ronseal was applied liberally all over. This was then left for 24 hours to sink in and dry. The surface was then lightly sanded with a fine sandpaper before a further coat of undiluted Ronseal was applied.

The table was again left for 24 hours before it was polished with a wax polish.

65. The finished table.

65

Veneered Commode

This mahogany veneered step commode was in good condition and complete with its liner. However it was painted all over in brown paint which lowered its value.

Stripping

As this piece of furniture was covered with veneer it could not be stripped by a method involving water and it was therefore decided to give it to a professional tank stripper to handle using a cold solvent process. This successfully removed all the paint without loosening the veneer.

66. *The commode as it arrived.*

67. *After stripping.*

68. *Applying stain to the mahogany veneer.*

67

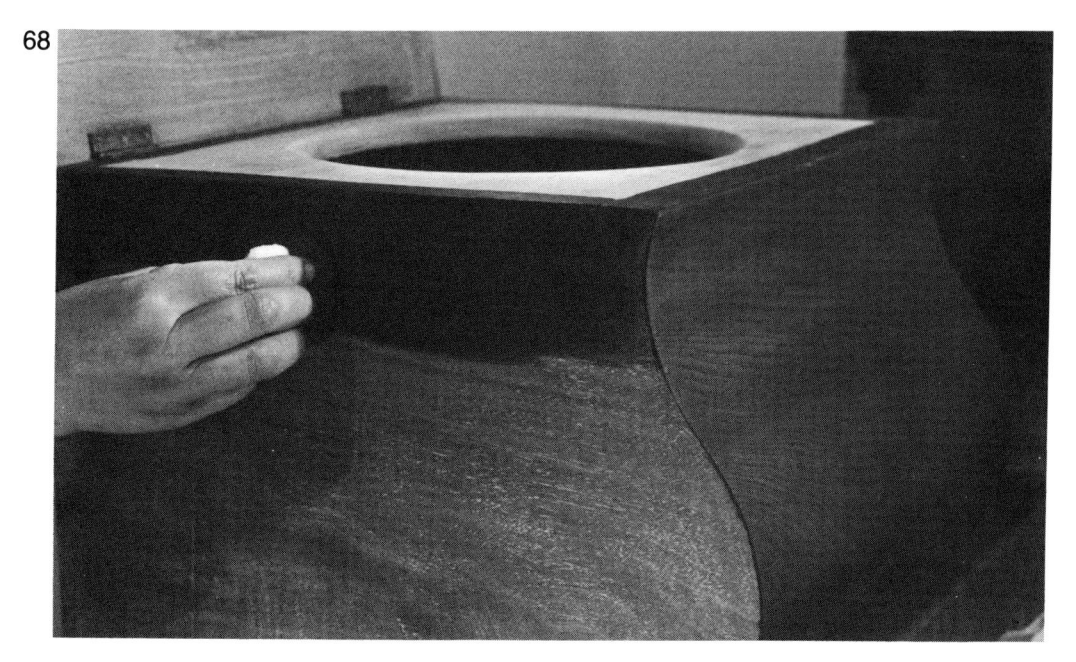

68

83

Restoration

During the stripping process the carpeting on the step and the commode, which was already in a bad condition, came away from the wood. This was replaced with an attractive and suitable material.

Rubbing Down

As the mahogany was still in good condition after stripping and drying, it was possible to smooth it successfully using only a fine wirewool. It was then necessary to stain it in order to regain the dark colour required.

Polishing

Once the stain was dry the wood was polished with a wax polish to obtain a very pleasing result.

69. After staining and polishing the commode had been returned to its original attractive condition.

69

Umbrella Stand

This umbrella stand was made of cast iron and had been painted several times in white and black paint. The two dishes at the base were removable.

Stripping

Some of the metal work was quite intricate and it would be difficult to clean out all the paint. Metal cannot warp and there is no glue to soften but if left wet metal does of course rust so care still has to be taken. The paint was removed by dipping the piece in a hot caustic tank.

Polishing

After stripping the metal was quite clear of paint so it was only necessary to polish it by applying black lead with a brush and polishing it vigorously with a brush and cloth to bring up the shine. This resulted in a most attractive piece which well repaid the work done on it.

70. The umbrella stand before any work was done on it – painted and in a bad condition.

71. The completed job – a relatively easy job and a pleasing result.

70

71

87

Handles and Brasswork

It may be that the furniture to be stripped has suitable handles and metal fixings and in this case it is only a matter of cleaning them. However it quite often happens that the original handles have either been lost or replaced by quite unsuitable plastic ones.

Both wooden handles and reproduction brass handles can be obtained to-day but these will need some treatment in order to blend with the old wood.

Wooden handles

If you are adept at carpentry it is not difficult to turn new handles on a lathe to match any existing handles. If you are not a carpenter new wooden handles can be bought and glued into place using G clamps.

Brasswork

New brass handles are very bright and obvious when purchased compared with the old handles which have had years of wear from use and from the atmosphere. Some may also have been lacquered and this should be removed with paint stripper before treatment.

In order to remove the bright surface we treat handles with ammonia fumes. This is done by placing the brasswork in a sealable container with a small pot of ammonia. The fumes given off will affect the brass and 'wear' the surface.

Be careful *not* to put the handles into the ammonia itself and do not leave them in the fumes for so long that they are damaged. The length of time will depend on the effect which you are seeking but we usually find about ten hours is sufficient before removing from the fumes and repolishing. Be very careful of thin brass items as these can disintegrate if left in the fumes for too long.

72. The sealed glass jar containing a paste pot of ammonia and a brass handle.

72

Doors

It may not be quite correct to include doors in a book entitled 'Stripping and polishing Furniture' but it is often necessary to strip doors so that they tone in with the stripped furniture. For this reason we feel that it is fair to stretch a point and include the subject.

The method used to strip a door can be any of those described earlier in this book. The jelly or paste strippers can be used or the hot air paintstripper, but if a hand method is used remember:

1. If the wood grain of the door has been filled the hot air paintstripper will not remove it.
2. Doors are a large area to strip by hand so beware of leaving patches due to areas not properly covered with the stripping agent.

Stripping in a tank is probably more often used for doors than hand stripping. This is because of the large areas of wood needing attention. However one should be aware that:

1. The door has, of course, to be taken down at the hinges and during the stripping porcess it is likely to expand or contract a little. Some rubbing down may therefore be required when refitting the door.
2. As with tank stripped furniture it may take several days before the door in dry enough to sand and polish.
3. Glass (but not mirror glass) can remain in the door while it is tank stripped. However professional strippers are unlikely to give a guarantee that the glass with not be damaged during the process because of the difficulty of handling wet and slippery wood.

In the case of both hand stripping or tank stripping if door handles, hooks, plates etc.

73. A door in the stripping tank.

74. Pressure hosing the doors to remove paint after they have been taken out of the tank.

73

74

have been painted over these should be taken off the door. They can be stripped in a solution of 1 ounce of caustic soda to 1 pint of water. But do not let caustic soda come into contact with aluminium which may be on doors in the form of handles or double glazing; these will certainly be damaged by the solution.

When tank stripping it is best to remove the knobs and handles to prevent damage in the tank although hinges can be left on the door.

In some cases, which are very rare, there can be a re-action between the solution in the stripping tank and a combination of a certain wood and a particular polish. This results in a furry surface being left on the wood which is difficult to remove. Do not blame the stripper if you have put the door out to a professional as there is no way he can fortell that this will happen. But of course it would be wise not to strip any more doors from the same house is this way.

Once the door has been stripped and is again dry it should be sanded or rubbed down with wirewool until it is suitably smooth. Next seal the wood with a clear polyurethane in the same way as you seal a table top, as the door will have to withstand quite a lot of handling, kicks and bumps. Then wax polish using, if you like, a fine wirewool to cut back the polyurethane a little and thin down the polish.

All that we have said above applies to doors made of pine. But if you are lucky enough to have a hardwood door to strip then it must to treated in the same way as stripping hardwood furniture. Water is likely to blacken it therefore making it necessary to use a non-waterbased solution to strip away the paint; otherwise the process is basically the same with maybe some stain added to revitalise the colour of the wood if it is required.

75. Stripped doors drying in the rack.

75

Some Suppliers Addresses

Brasswork Suppliers:

J. D. Beardmore & Co. Ltd.
3 Percy Street,
London W.1.

Wirewool is available from hardware stores. Wirewool on reels is sometimes more difficult to obtain. A good brand is marketed by:

J. W. Bollom & Co. Ltd.
P.O. Box 78,
Beckenham,
Kent.

Tank stripping service using the cold solvent system:

Lift-Off,
Wealden Forest Park,
Herne Common,
Herne Bay,
Kent.
Tel: 0227 712551

Wax polishes in various shades should be available from hardware stores. Briwax is manufactured by:

J. W. Bollom & Co. Ltd.
P.O. Box 78,
Beckenham,
Kent.

Veneers, boxwood and **stringing** for use when restoring furniture

J. Crispin & Sons Ltd.,
92–96, Curtain Road,
Shorditch,
London E.C.2

Index

Black lead	86
Bleaching	44
Burns	44
Brasswork	88
Brummer stopping	8
Caustic Soda	36
Cling film	20
Coid solvent	38
Doors	90
Drum Sander	10
Emulsion paint	28
Evo-stick Resin W	8
Fillers	8
Filling trowel	6
G clamps	8
Handles	88
Hot air paintstripper	22
Jellied stripper	16
Mole clamp	52

Nails	46
Nail set	8
Nitromors	18
Orbital sander	10
Paint stripper	16
Polishing	66
Regluing	48
Ronseal	64
Ronstrip	20
Sanding	64
Sash clamps	8
Scraping tools	6
Sealing	64
Shave hook	6
Stain	44
Tack lifter	8
Tinted polish	66
Wirewool	6, 10
Wood dye or stain	44
Woodworm killer	8
Woodworm treatment	50